The Story of
The Ten Commandments

The Story of
The Ten Commandments

WRITTEN BY PATRICIA A. PINGRY • ILLUSTRATED BY STACY VENTURI-PICKETT

ideals children's books™
NASHVILLE, TENNESSEE

ISBN-13: 978-0-8249-5554-0
ISBN-10: 0-8249-5554-4

Published by Ideals Children's Books
An imprint of Ideals Publications
A Guideposts Company
535 Metroplex Drive, Suite 250
Nashville, Tennessee 37211
www.idealsbooks.com

Library of Congress CIP data on file

Color separations by Precision Color Graphics, Franklin, Wisconsin

Printed and bound in Italy by LEGO

10 9 8 7 6 5 4 3 2 1

For Nicholas

This book belongs to

_____

From

_____

Do you follow rules at home and school? God gave us rules too. We call God's rules the Ten Commandments.

God
first gave His rules
to the Israelites,
who were slaves in
Egypt.

One day, God spoke to Moses through a burning bush. God told Moses to lead the Israelites to a new land and freedom.

God
held back the
waters of the sea.
The Israelites
walked out of
Egypt
to freedom.

God took care of
His people. He sent
food, called
manna,
for them to eat.

One day
God
called Moses
to come
to the top of
Mount Sinai.

Moses walked
UP,
UP,
UP
until he was at the
top of the mountain.
Then Moses
met God.

Moses could not
see God.
God was hidden
in a thick
cloud.
But Moses heard
God.

God wrote
ten rules on
two stone tablets.
We call these the
Ten
Commandments.

These are
God's rules:

1. There is only
one God.
2. Bow down to no one
but God.
3. Speak God's name
with respect.
4. Give one day each
week to God.
5. Respect your parents.

6. Do not kill.

7. Be faithful to your family.

8. Do not steal.

9. Do not lie.

10. Do not want what others have.

These are God's
Ten
Commandments.
These are the
rules
we follow at school
and at play.